THE LITTLE
INSTRUCTION
BOOK FOR
CATS

THE LITTLE INSTRUCTION BOOK FOR CATS

This revised edition copyright © Summersdale Publishers Ltd, 2018
First published in 2014

Research by Malcolm Croft

Illustrations by Dannyboy

An Hachette UK Company
www.hachette.co.uk

Summersdale Publishers Ltd
Part of Octopus Publishing Group Limited
Carmelite House
50 Victoria Embankment
LONDON
EC4Y 0DZ

www.summersdale.com

Printed and bound in China

ISBN: 978-1-78685-534-3

THE LITTLE
INSTRUCTION
BOOK FOR
CATS

BOXES ARE GREAT FUN. BUT BEFORE YOU JUMP IN,
MAKE SURE YOU HAVE AN EXIT STRATEGY.

DANNYBOY
AND **KATE FREEMAN**

summersdale

In ancient times, cats were worshipped as gods; they have not forgotten this.

TERRY PRATCHETT

INTRODUCTION

Eat. Sleep. Stretch. Repeat. Human beings think that being a cat is so easy. But it's not. Being a cat involves a lot of hard work – constant licking and purring, stretching and scratching, cleaning and clawing. It's not all fun and games and, despite being mankind's real best friend (move along dogs), there is no instruction manual for how to be a Top Cat… until now!

The Little Instruction Book For Cats is your ultimate companion, guaranteed to teach you all you need to know to become a better cat: a cat that not only gets the cream, but the entire pavlova.

INSTRUCTION No. 1

DRINKS ON TABLE SURFACES ARE THERE TO BE KNOCKED OFF. THIS IS YOUR DUTY.

INSTRUCTION No. 2

DOOR STOPPERS – YOU KNOW, THE SPRINGY THINGS THAT MAKE THAT FUNNY BA-DOINNNNGG! NOISE – SHOULD BE PLAYED WITH AT APPROXIMATELY 2 A.M. EVERY NIGHT. WHEN A FAMILY MEMBER COMES AND TELLS YOU TO STOP, TAKE THE OPPORTUNITY TO RUN INTO THE BEDROOM AND LIE IN THE MIDDLE OF THEIR BED.

INSTRUCTION NO. 3

DON'T BOTHER CHASING MICE. IT'S TOO MUCH
LIKE HARD WORK. INSTEAD, BEFRIEND THEM,
PLAY WITH THEM, LULL THEM INTO A FALSE
SENSE OF SECURITY AND THEN WHEN THEY
THINK THEY ARE SAFE, EAT THEM.

INSTRUCTION No. 4

AFTER A HARD DAY AT WORK, THE FAMILY WILL
WANT TO VENT THEIR FRUSTRATIONS AT YOU.
MAKE YOURSELF SCARCE BETWEEN 5.30 P.M. AND
7 P.M. STROLL IN NONCHALANTLY AT DINNER TIME
WHEN THE ATMOSPHERE IS A BIT MORE CHILLED.

INSTRUCTION No.5

NEVER GET WET. NEVER EVER GET WET.
NEVER EVER EVER GET WET!

INSTRUCTION No. 6

MAKING LOTS OF NOISE AND DISTURBING THE
NEIGHBOURS IN THE MIDDLE OF THE NIGHT IS
ALWAYS GOOD FUN. BEST ACHIEVED BY CRASHING
AROUND IN THE GARDEN AND CLATTERING IN AND
OUT THROUGH THE CAT FLAP AT LIGHTNING SPEED.

INSTRUCTION No. 7

IF A FAMILY MEMBER IS WORKING ON
THEIR COMPUTER, THE BEST WAY TO GET
THEIR ATTENTION (AND AFFECTION) IS TO
LIE DOWN ON TOP OF THE KEYBOARD.

INSTRUCTION No. 8

YOUR FAMILY WILL BUY YOU A SCRATCHING POST. THIS IS THEIR WAY OF TRYING TO CONTROL WHERE YOU DO ALL YOUR SCRATCHING. IGNORE IT. IT JUST DOESN'T QUITE DO THE JOB AS WELL AS THEIR EXPENSIVE LEATHER SOFAS AND ORNATE, HEIRLOOM WOODEN FURNITURE.

INSTRUCTION No. 9

YOUR FAMILY ARE FOREVER ON THEIR PHONES
THESE DAYS. IF YOU WANT SOME AFFECTION WHILE
SOMEONE'S ON THE PHONE YOU HAVE TO GET
CREATIVE. TRY LYING ON TOP OF ANY PHONES
THAT ARE LEFT LYING AROUND (BONUS: IT'LL
BE NICE AND WARM FROM BEING USED SO MUCH)
AND SMILE SMUGLY TO YOURSELF WHEN THEY
ASK 'HAS ANYONE SEEN MY PHONE?'

INSTRUCTION No. 10

WOOLLY JUMPERS ARE GREAT FUN, ESPECIALLY IF THEY HAVE BEEN KNITTED BY ONE OF THE FAMILY. THEY MAY HAVE TAKEN HOURS TO MAKE, BUT THEY TAKE HALF AS LONG TO UNRAVEL. PLUS, ONCE YOU START, YOU CAN'T STOP!

NEVER DRINK FROM YOUR WATER BOWL —
IT'S TOO CLOSE TO YOUR LITTER BOX, YUCK! AND
YOU NEVER KNOW WHAT'S BEEN IN THAT TOILET
WATER RECENTLY. ALWAYS DRINK FRESH WATER
FROM A DRIPPING TAP IN THE KITCHEN SINK.

INSTRUCTION No. 12

A GOOD WAY TO MAKE ROOM FOR DINNER IS
TO HACK UP THE HAIR YOU ATE FOR LUNCH.
IT'S EVEN MORE FUN IF YOU LEAVE THEM IN
STRATEGIC PLACES FOR YOUR HUMAN TO FIND.

INSTRUCTION NO.13

IF A BEDROOM DOOR IS SHUT, CLAW AT IT
VIOLENTLY UNTIL SOMEONE OPENS IT, NO
MATTER WHAT IT IS YOU MAY BE INTERRUPTING.

INSTRUCTION No. 14

DRAUGHT EXCLUDERS ARE NOT SNAKES.
BUT THEY ARE FUN TO DESTROY.

INSTRUCTION No. 15

TV CABLES — ANY LOOSE WIRES, IN FACT —
SHOULD BE PULLED UNTIL YOU HEAR A LOUD NOISE.
IT'LL KEEP YOUR HUMANS BUSY FOR A FEW HOURS
SO YOU CAN GET SOME PEACE AND QUIET.

INSTRUCTION No. 16

TOILET PAPER IS THE TOY THAT KEEPS ON GIVING.
DON'T STOP PLAYING WITH THE TOILET PAPER
UNTIL YOU SEE THE CARDBOARD ROLL!

INSTRUCTION No. 17

SHOPPING BAGS, FRESHLY BROUGHT INTO THE HOUSE, REQUIRE INSPECTION IMMEDIATELY. IF THIS INVOLVES GETTING IN THE BAG, THEN SO BE IT.

INSTRUCTION No.18

JUST BECAUSE YOU DON'T NEED TO BE WALKED – LIKE A DOG – DOESN'T MEAN YOU DON'T NEED EXERCISE. THANKFULLY, JUMPING UP AND DOWN ON A SOCK FOR TEN MINUTES AND CHEWING ON A HAIR-TIE IS CONSIDERED EXERCISE.

INSTRUCTION No. 19

IF YOU'RE GOING TO STICK YOUR HEAD INTO A
TIN OF CAT FOOD — TO LICK THE BITS AT THE
BOTTOM — DON'T PUSH IT ALL THE WAY IN.

INSTRUCTION No. 20

IF YOU NEED TO GIVE YOURSELF A GOOD LICK AFTER A PARTICULARLY DIRTY DAY IN THE GARDEN, DO IT IN FULL VIEW OF THE FAMILY – IDEALLY ON THE DINING-ROOM TABLE WHILE EVERYBODY IS EATING.

INSTRUCTION No. 21

IT IS ENTERTAINING TO WAIT UNTIL YOU
SENSE YOUR HUMAN IS ROUSING FROM THEIR
COMFY SPOT ON THE SOFA – PROBABLY TO GO
TO THE LOO – TO LIE ADORABLY ON THEIR LAP.

YOUR HUMANS DRINK WATER FROM GLASSES.
SHOW YOUR LOVE FOR THEM BY SHARING
THEIR WATER WITH THEM.

INSTRUCTION No. 23

CHRISTMAS TREES ARE FUN TO CLIMB UP
AND KNOCK OVER. THE HIGHER YOU CAN
CLIMB, THE BETTER THE CAT YOU ARE. ALL
ORNAMENTS ARE TO BE DESTROYED!

INSTRUCTION No. 24

SHOW YOUR HUMANS HOW BAD THEIR
TASTE IN TOYS IS BY THROWING ANY
YOU DON'T LIKE IN THE TOILET.

INSTRUCTION No. 25

WHENEVER ANYTHING MOVES UNDERNEATH
A BLANKET YOU MUST ATTACK IT UNTIL IT
DIES. YOUR BELOVED HUMAN IS UNDERNEATH
THERE AND NEEDS PROTECTING FROM
THE EVIL MOVING THINGS.

INSTRUCTION No. 26

TAKE RANDOM OBJECTIONS TO FOODS
YOU'VE PREVIOUSLY ENJOYED, JUST TO
KEEP YOUR HUMANS ON THEIR TOES.

YOU DON'T WANT YOUR HUMAN'S ATTENTION,
BUT YOU ALSO DON'T THINK IT'S RIGHT
THAT YOUR HUMAN SHOULD GIVE THEIR
ATTENTION TO ANYTHING ELSE. SIT ON
WHATEVER IT IS THEY'RE OCCUPIED
WITH AND THEN IGNORE THEM.

IT'S IMPORTANT TO REMEMBER THAT AS SOON
AS YOU'VE BEEN LET OUTSIDE, YOU SHOULD
INSTANTLY START HOWLING TO BE LET BACK IN.
IT'S JUST NOT FUN OTHERWISE.

INSTRUCTION NO. 29

HUMANS ARE LAZY AND SLEEP FOR FAR TOO LONG AT NIGHT-TIME. THEY'LL BE INCREDIBLY GRATEFUL IF YOU TAKE TO WAKING THEM UP (PERHAPS BY LYING ON THEIR FACE) ABOUT AN HOUR BEFORE THEIR ALARM GOES OFF.

INSTRUCTION No. 30

IF YOU'RE SMALL ENOUGH TO FIT IN A HANDBAG
OR A SHOE, GO FOR IT. SMALL PLACES ARE EXTRA
COSY! REMEMBER THE GOLDEN RULE: IF YOUR
WHISKERS TOUCH THE SIDES, IT'S A
GOOD PLACE TO HIDE.

INSTRUCTION No. 31

IF THERE ARE MULTIPLE LAPS AVAILABLE
FOR SITTING ON (SAY YOUR HUMANS HAVE
GUESTS OVER), THE BEST LAP TO SIT ON
ALWAYS BELONGS TO THE PERSON WHO IS
PURPOSELY STARING IN THE OPPOSITE
DIRECTION TO YOU, COVERING THEMSELVES
WITH THEIR ARMS AND LOOKING PANICKY.

INSTRUCTION No. 32

ONLY GO NEAR A VACUUM CLEANER THAT
IS QUIET. NEVER TRUST A NOISY ONE.

INSTRUCTION No. 33

IF YOU'RE GOING TO WATCH THE BIRDS IN THE GARDEN FROM THE COMFORT OF THE INDOORS, REMEMBER THERE IS A WINDOW BETWEEN YOU AND THEM. CLAWING AT THE WINDOW WILL NOT HARM THE BIRDS IN ANY WAY, BUT PRESSING YOUR FACE UP AGAINST IT MIGHT GIVE THEM A GOOD SCARE!

SHOW OFF HOW STATELY, PROUD AND BEAUTIFUL YOU ARE BY STRETCHING OUT ACROSS THE HALLWAY, FLAUNTING YOUR FINE FIGURE AND MAKING THE HUMANS STEP OVER YOU EVERY TIME THEY NEED TO MOVE AROUND THE HOUSE.

INSTRUCTION No. 35

WHEN YOUR OWNER IS GETTING READY FOR WORK IN THE MORNING, THE BEST PIECE OF REAL ESTATE IN THE HOUSE IS ON TOP OF THEIR CLEAN, NEWLY IRONED, WARM AND EXTRA-SOFT CLOTHES.

YOUR FAMILY MAY NOT NOTICE IF YOU'RE FEELING UNWELL, SO YOU'VE GOT TO MAKE IT REALLY OBVIOUS BY ACTING OUT OF CHARACTER IN AS MANY WAYS AS YOU CAN THINK OF. BEING AFFECTIONATE AND WELL-BEHAVED IS A SURE-FIRE WAY TO ROUSE THEIR SUSPICIONS.

INSTRUCTION No. 37

IF YOU FIND A DEAD MOUSE (BEHIND A SKIRTING BOARD OR KITCHEN CUPBOARD), RUN AROUND THE HOUSE DRAMATICALLY FOR A BIT AND THEN SHOW EVERYBODY YOUR 'CATCH' — YOU'LL GET MORE PRAISE AND ATTENTION FOR CATCHING A LIVE MOUSE THAN FOR SIMPLY FINDING A DEAD ONE.

INSTRUCTION No.38

REMEMBER: MIRRORS ARE NOT OTHER CATS.

INSTRUCTION No. 39

EVERY TIME A MEMBER OF THE FAMILY GOES
TO THE TOILET, FOLLOW THEM IN AND STARE
AT THEM. THIS WILL MAKE THEM FEEL
INCREDIBLY UNCOMFORTABLE AND PUT
THEM OFF. THIS IS VERY GOOD FUN.

IF YOU GET STUCK WHILE EXPLORING, DON'T WORRY, YOU DON'T NEED TO GET YOURSELF OUT OF THE MESS ON YOUR OWN: JUST CATERWAUL UNTIL YOUR HUMAN COMES AND RESCUES YOU.

INSTRUCTION No. 41

EXPOSED, SHOE-LESS FEET ARE FOR ATTACKING.

INSTRUCTION No. 42

FROM TIME TO TIME IT'S FUN TO HAVE A STARING
CONTEST WITH YOUR HUMANS. THEY'LL SPEND AGES
TRYING TO WORK OUT WHAT YOU'RE TRYING TO
COMMUNICATE, AND MAY EVEN GIVE YOU TREATS
TO SEE IF THAT SORTS YOU OUT.

HUMANS ARE ONLY ALLOWED TO RUB YOUR BELLY
A PRECISE, PRE-CHOSEN AND ALWAYS-CHANGING
NUMBER OF TIMES BEFORE YOU CLAW THEM.
THIS KEEPS THEM ON THEIR TOES.

WHEN YOUR FAMILY GOES AWAY FOR THE DAY,
THE HOUSE IS YOUR KINGDOM. INVITE FRIENDS
THROUGH THE CAT FLAP FOR A PARTY. RUN RIOT
IN THE HOUSE. WHILE THE HUMANS ARE
AWAY THE CATS CAN PLAY!

INSTRUCTION No. 45

BOXES ARE GREAT FUN. BUT BEFORE
YOU JUMP IN, MAKE SURE YOU HAVE
AN EXIT STRATEGY.

If you're interested in finding out more
about our books, find us on Facebook at
SUMMERSDALE PUBLISHERS and follow us
on Twitter at @SUMMERSDALE.

WWW.SUMMERSDALE.COM